FEAR - Face Everything And Rise
My journey to living in joy and leading with love
By Bernadette Trafton

Introduction

This is my journey into learning how to live life in joy and making a decision that caused me to always lead with love. I haven't always been in alignment with this focus. I struggled a lot and during a portion of my life I lived in misery. I wasn't always as in love with life as I am as I write this. I sought out other's approval of me more than I listened to myself. Through it all I learned to face everything and rise. Trust me, if I can get to where I am today, you can too! Implementing just a few practical things in your life, can bring you there too. I've had many teachers along way. Some of them good, some of them bad, all of them I'm grateful for because of the amazing journey I've had.

I will share the key things I've learned and how you can create abundance in your life, create the life of your dreams. The beauty is it's a universal law. When you live in joy and lead with love, you increase your vibrational frequency to draw to you every experience and any amount of abundance you desire. Oftentimes, this requires you leave behind the identity you have in your mind of who you are as a person. I hear so often, "But, Bernadette, that's not who I AM!" I respond, "So what, if who you are is not who you want to be, if where you are at, is not where you want to be. You will need to make some changes to move from where you are to where you want to be. As one of my teachers always said, if nothing changes, nothing changes. If you don't change, then nothing changes." In order to change it will require you to not only step outside your comfort zone, you will need to live outside your comfort zone. It's ok, I promise, it's pretty magical here. And, the beauty and power is, you have the ability to create whomever you want to be and whatever you want in your life.

This book is segmented into a few parts. The first part of the book is an introduction to my teachers. I think it's important that you meet some of the people who have helped form my life. It's my hope through the stories I share and the teachers I introduce you to, you learn that we have the ability to create our lives. With this knowledge we are able to manifest anything we want in our lives. I will share the secrets in the pages that follow my stories. It's my desire these stories will also bring you some of the joy I have in my life.

What we cover will help you get into alignment with your true purpose. Please understand, what that looks like will be different for every person reading this book. We are all unique. What brings us into joy and gets our proverbial "juices" flowing is going to be different for every person. So, make a promise to me right now that you will not compare yourself to me or to anyone else. Promise me, particularly when we get into the practical applications, that the only voice you will listen to is your own. And, I encourage you to not read ahead. Don't just go to the practical applications. It is my belief as you learn about my teachers, you will learn about me. And, as you learn about me, you will realize, though our goals may be different, we are not so different. And, if I can create my life in a way that brings me joy and abundance, you too will be able to create your life in ways that bring you everything you've ever wanted in life.

With joy in my heart, much love and appreciation,

Bernadette Trafton, Chief Connector, Master of Meditation and Soul Sister

My first teacher, Oma

Oma

Oma was/is my mother, Ursula. Everyone called her Oma. She was my first, most listened to, most confided in teacher and is also my first experience of someone who lived with her heart on her sleeve. She was the most loving, giving person I've ever known in my life. The first time I met her, she was 31 years old. I'm sure she wasn't expecting to have a 5th child, but, after having 4 boys, the dream of having a girl, I'm sure, thrilled her. She was always making beautiful clothes, knitting, crocheting sweaters or embroidering store bought clothes to 'spiff them up'.

Whether she would admit it or not, she was always an entrepreneur and instilled that passion in me. I think she really wanted her own money to do with what she wanted whenever she felt like doing it. For me, that notion always meant freedom. I remember when I was little and we lived in Georgia, she owned a yarn store, The Yarn Shop. She and my Aunt Christa would hold knitting classes, crocheting classes, macramé classes and more. There is so much joy in creating and watching others create. As I look back at my lineage, I definitely got the entrepreneur spirit from my mother's side of the family. My Godmother, Tante Erika (Mom's Sister) owned a yarn shop in NJ. My Opa Ebbers (Mom's Dad) owned a restaurant in Germany the whole family worked at. My Uncle Peter owned a restaurant with his wife. I think at some point in their lives, most of her siblings ran some sort of a business.

My afternoons after school were often spent at The Yarn Shop, learning how to make items with my hands. I remember the Chinese food restaurant next door. The lady loved my Mom and I would often go there and eat something yummy or even better learn how to make something.

We often made these amazing rice-type balls. I don't remember what they were called, all I

know is you had to be very gentle with them or they would flatten out. I remember loving the

egg drop soup and having soy sauce on my rice. And, I remember the feeling of community.

Our lives kind of changed when I was 8. We were called up to NH when my Grandmother

(Dad's Mom) had multiple heart attacks and passed away. I will never forget it. It was Easter

Sunday; we had just buried my Grandmother and my father had a heart attack. Back then, the

doctors wouldn't allow you to travel when you survived a heart attack. So, we moved to NH

from Georgia. I remember hearing about my Grandmother. How wonderful she was. She was

always helping people. She was a nurse by trade and, she would come home at night and not

only cook for her family, she cooked for neighborhood families in need. Oma always said,

"When we went to your Grandmother's for a holiday, the family couldn't eat until the neighbors

in need ate. Your Grandmother would cook several dinners and then she would put it all in

serving dishes and deliver the meals to local families. Before she left to deliver the food, she

would get everyone moving on cooking the meal we would eventually eat." The stories of my

Grandmother were a lesson in kindness and love for people without the cloud of judgement that

is often spewed in today's culture. But I digress.

Quickly after we moved to NH, Oma's entrepreneur spirit kicked in again. She was always

making some sort of a craft and always got us kids to pitch in. She worked so hard. She worked

as a waitress, usually second shift and the rest of the time she was making crafts. She was

always busy, always moving and I don't really remember her taking time for herself when we were kids. She would find local craft fairs and almost every weekend during craft fair season we would be selling her creations and selling our own. I learned some of my best lessons in business and life from my mother. Even so, I remember always thinking, I want my Mother's heart and her passion for people, but I don't want her life. She worked so hard all of the time. There has to be an easier path. I remember having conversations with my brother Marcus, who you will meet later in this book. We always said, there has to be an easier way.

As I got older, I followed Oma's passion for people. I worked at nursing homes and in my early twenties began working in a group home with kids who had been pulled from their homes for a variety of reasons. The lessons I'd learned from my mother and the stories of my Grandmother allowed me to bring compassion and caring, without judgement, in this setting. However, I also learned very quickly, in this field, you don't make much money, which meant life could be hard. In order to make the money you wanted to make, you had to trade more of your time for money. This left little to no time to live life and explore on your own terms. I didn't realize it at the time, but, the real reason I walked away from this profession was because it wasn't in alignment with my purpose and the lifestyle I wanted to live. So, I moved on to what I knew best which was being an entrepreneur.

We decided we were going to start a polar fleece clothing company. We didn't really know how we were going to do it. We just knew that we were going to do it. Funny thing is when you know your why and give it to God, amazing things can happen. We foraged for the best fleece at Malden Mills in Lawrence and began creating designs. It was a joyous time. We had moved into my brother Steve's home to help him with his son Zachary. Zack was always a curious child. And, like Oma, he was always making something. We called him the tape master. He was always creating something because he was with Oma all the time, who was always creating something. It's a beautiful thing to watch children in this mode. They are so uninhibited. They do what feels right to them. There's a lesson there that I will talk about later in the book.

We quickly found ourselves back at the fairs with our polar fleece business, but this time on a different scale. I wanted to do things differently. I packed up a sales kit with sample garments and I started meeting stores to sell items wholesale, went to schools and white-water rafting companies to sell logo wear, began a home party business and opened a store front in a little over a year. It's amazing what type of inspiration you can find when you give yourself time to create. And, we were having so much fun. We were pretty successful for quite a while. And, then we faced some market struggles after 5 years in business and we decided to throw in the towel. I know now there was a possibility in the universe to have kept that business running and make it wildly successful. I just didn't know it at the time.

During the years that followed, my mother went through my most trying relationships with me. I won't get into much detail about those relationships. I'm sure everyone has their own perception of events. The best is that I learned lessons about how to recognize what I didn't want in my life from each of them. The worst is I allowed them to make me feel ugly, fat, useless and unworthy. At the time I believed everything they told me about who I was as a person. Looking back, all I can be is grateful to them because I have a beautiful daughter and a beautiful son. Oma was there for all of it. She was my best friend, my confidante, oftentimes roommate. I love her dearly.

At the tail end of the second relationship with my son's father, I was in my late thirties and I knew I wanted to be a stay at home Mom. I wasn't really sure how I would make this happen. I just knew it had to happen. I saw a movie about this woman who left her corporate career and made a huge company making apple sauce. It inspired me to learn how to make jams and chutneys and I quickly began making jam and selling it at farmer's markets. Oma was living over an hour away from us, but she came down at least once a week to go to one of the 5 farmer's markets I went to. She, of course, brought her crafts that she'd been making. We had so much fun at those markets. We had a blast chatting with people and we had regulars who would come all the time.

We, of course, started doing craft fairs again. She never charged enough money. Sometimes, I swear she would make things for craft fairs for the sole purpose of giving away gifts of joy to people. A little girl would come up and fall in love with a doll and Oma would just give it to her. A little boy would come up and want the Jester hat she made and if his parents didn't buy it for him, she would give it to him. I know she received just as much joy in the giving as the people who were receiving. I still go to craft fairs, and if I'm quiet, I can hear Oma, *"Oh, I could make that"*, *"Vow, that's really beautiful"*, one time I heard, *"Look she does nice work and the price is so low, she is basically giving it away, buy 3"*. I, of course bought 3.

When the relationship with my son's father basically blew up, I got the sense that making jam wasn't going to support me and 2 kids. Time taught me quickly that I wouldn't get regular child support to help. I knew for certain that I didn't want to go back to work in a traditional sense. I knew I wanted to be a stay at home mom who was able to provide by working from home. I didn't want my children to be raised by anyone other than me. The only way I could do that was to work from home and work for myself. At that point, I made the decision to be an entrepreneur for the rest of my life. Oma supported me along the way even though she didn't understand my business choices. I jumped head-first into real estate and network marketing. I met so many teachers and my life-long mentor along the way. You will meet many of them in the following pages. I also made the decision to really get to know me.

This was a long process. I'm not sure when it happened, but at some point, I decided not to seek out a relationship. I remember having conversations with Oma. She would always tell me how amazing I was. But, something in me told me I wasn't happy enough with me to offer anything real in a relationship. I didn't trust myself. I used to tell myself I had a bad picker. What I realize as I'm typing this, is I didn't trust my own feelings. I always let the man's feelings guide the relationship. I always asked myself the question, *"What can I do to make this person happy with me."* I realize now, I never asked myself, *"How do I feel when I'm with this person?"*

As I jumped into real estate and network marketing many things began happening, quickly. I was approached at a meeting to start my own real estate investors association. At first, I shied away from the idea because I didn't feel like I knew enough. I learned in network marketing you could "sponsor your weakness" so I teamed up with Ann, who knew far more about real estate than I did. I talked to Oma about whether she thought I could accomplish the goal. I just remember her looking at me and saying, *"You can create anything you want, Bernadette!"* That was all I needed. So many people told me I was nuts and crazy whether it was about this real estate investors association or whether it was about network marketing. But it didn't matter. I knew my 'Why' and I knew the 'HOW' would present itself. Even Ann told me most associations like this start small with a few people in them, so we would have to invest our own money. I didn't know how at the time, but I said to her, *"No, we will have over 100 members and over $10,000 in the bank from membership sales before we even have our first meeting!"* I marketed everywhere it was possible to market at the time and in the end, we had 125 members and over $12,000 in the bank when we opened the doors for the first meeting. Ann and I parted ways after a few years. It's amazing we got along as long as we did. Ann used to describe our relationship in this way, *"Bernadette is the winged unicorn flying around in the sky chasing ideas and dreams and I'm on the ground with my foot in the mud grabbing her tail and pulling her back down to earth."* It's hard to fly when you've got someone pulling you down to earth. And I'm sure Ann got tired of trying.

I guess the real point in this story is that Oma believed I could accomplish anything I wanted to. I borrowed her belief in me, and magic happened. Oma was a blessing to everyone she met. And, if they paid attention, they would learn so much from her. I didn't recognize all the lessons until later in our journey together and I recognized even more after she passed on. I don't believe in regrets. I believe we learn along the way. I'm a Taurus and at times I have lived up to the notion of being a bull. Oma said I was hard at times. When she said it, it just upset me, but, in retrospect, she was right. I wasn't always kind to her. I was oftentimes a bull because it was more important for me to be right than it was to lead with love and at times, I acted ungrateful for all she did for me. She and my kids have taught me the greatest lessons in unconditional love I have ever known. Even with that unconditional love, I didn't know how to live in joy, live in gratitude or even what the concept of leading with love was. At the time, I didn't realize the most important person I needed to fall in love with was me. I know that Oma knew that. The last few years of her life were physically difficult. She had an operation the doctors told her she needed, and her body just seemed to give up after that. I think the hardest thing for her was not being able to do everything she wanted to do. This was a woman who drove her car down into the fenced in back yard so she could put the trash in it because it was taking Zack too long to come do it for her. She despised relying on other people.

She told me that she didn't want to die in the hospital, and she asked me if she could be at home with me. How could I refuse? She lived her life on her own terms, and she wanted to die on her own terms. Saying goodbye to her was the hardest thing I've ever had to do in life. She was my mother, but she was so much more. And, my son and I sat in the living room while she slept watching Harry Potter of all things and we watched her take her last breath.

It took me a bit to find my spiritual connection to my mother. Not that she didn't try. One day Sebastian yelled down to me, *"Mom, Oma's playing video games with me!"* He snapped a picture of a little badass character named Ursula who was walking around in this virtual world he was on. When I had Comcast, the caller ID on the TV would say, "Receiving a call from Ursula Sasso and no one would be there when I answered the phone. I'm incredibly grateful to have that connection now because I know Oma is looking in on me and she loves my focus. She loves the title of this book. More importantly, she loves how I'm living my best life.

Annie

I met Annie at one of the REIA (real estate investors association) meetings I helped run before starting my own REIA and before starting my network marketing career. She was different than almost anyone I had ever met. She was always happy. She was always bouncing around and her energy was magnetic. She always had a tan. I remember watching her and I noticed she always complimented everyone. She would point out something about the person that someone else wouldn't have noticed. If they had a nice piece of jewelry or pretty blue eyes or a nice outfit, she would mention it. She has a charm focused on lifting people up.

I was in a rough place mentally when I first met Annie. I didn't believe in myself. I was still believing what those relationships left me to believe about myself. I had no confidence. But Annie was always kind to me, so, one day I built up enough courage to ask, *"What exactly do you DO?"* She laughed and said, *"I show people how to make money. And, I'm not talking about trading your time for money. I'm talking about leverage and creating residual income. Money that comes in month after month after month for something you do right one time. So, you can live the life you want to live and wake up when your eyes open, not when the alarm clock goes off"* I said eagerly, *"Show me, please, I have 2 kids, I'm a single Mom and from the looks of things, I have no hope of getting child support."* That one conversation changed my life forever. Honestly, she could have been selling pencils and I would have joined her. She was pure joy and fun and I knew I wanted that in my life.

Annie taught me how important it is to not pre-judge other people. You never know their "why" or how they will be willing to change to achieve their goals. Most people would have looked at me and said, *"I'm not going to bother with that girl. She has no network, she has no self-esteem, she has nothing to bring to the table."* Not Annie. Annie was like the aunt in that amazing movie with Rosalind Russel, Auntie Mame. My brother Marcus and I used to watch it all the time. I still watch it and have seen it performed live a few different times. Auntie Mame says, *"Life is a banquet and most poor suckers are starving. So, live, live, live."*

Annie recognized that I had no believe in myself. But she knew that if I was able to borrow her belief in the systems, I might just begin to believe in myself. She also knew when that happened, I would be able to accomplish anything I wanted to. She taught me the importance of sharing your belief in others. Every opportunity she got she would build me up and tell me how amazing I was even when I felt like I could have done better. In that way, she is a lot like Oma.

I'll never forget an event we had, and the Owner/President Bill was going to be in attendance and speaking. I was so nervous. I had been inviting people for weeks. I had 10 people who had confirmed they were going to be there. I had never met Bill before. All I wanted to do was impress him. He was so successful, a real estate investor, restauranteur and he had created this business and system that was helping me to create a different lifestyle for me and my kids. My life had already changed so much. The night of the event, only 6 of the guests who had confirmed showed up. I was so embarrassed. I should have done more to make sure they were in the room. I almost didn't want to go up and meet him. On a side note, remember this, negative self-talk does nothing for you except taking you out of being open to receive the good that's coming. Annie said, *"Bernadette, you had 6 people show up, all 6 of them joined, focus on how amazing that is and not the duds who didn't show up, it's their loss."* Fear is a funny thing. There are many ways people look at it. They say fear is an acronym for false evidence appearing real. Some say, forget everything and run. With Annie's encouragement, I chose to face everything and rise. I wrangled up my courage and went up to meet Bill. Annie knew what I didn't know. Annie knew he would be thrilled with my guests and with me. I remember nervously saying, *"Only 6 of my 10 confirmed guests showed up."* He laughed and said, *"What you are doing here is amazing, Bernadette. Annie talks about you all the time. You have the potential to be a Rock star in this business. Go be a Rock star."* Wow, me be a rock star. I think that's when my unicorn started getting her wings.

My experiences with Annie have taught me so many lessons. She opened my eyes to the different ways to generate income. She taught me the importance of not trading your time for money. She taught me the importance of systems. But she really taught me not to pre-judge other people. And, sometimes you have to lend your belief to another person to help them believe in themselves. For that belief, I will always be grateful. Annie and I have made a lot of money together in this industry, we will always be friends and we chat all the time. Oh, and I see Bill on a weekly zoom meeting. They gave the best to me which helped me give the best of myself. And, where business is concerned, thanks to Oma, Annie and Bill, I began to believe in myself in ways that I'd never believed in myself before.

Dale

When I first started in my network marketing career, I met one of my teachers, Big Dawg, Dale Johnson. We lost him far too early. He's part of the reason I'm so focused on empowering other people. He always made it about the other person.

I remember meeting him at my first convention. I was building a team of people, and had some success, I think I had maybe 17 people on my team and had been in the business just over a few months. But I was the only person on my team that was at the convention and I was nervous because the only person I knew was Annie. Dale was this big teddy bear of a man. The first time I saw him, he was on stage sharing words of wisdom with a room full of thousands of people. The first time I actually met him was in the lobby area of the hotel during a break in between the afternoon session and dinner. I had told Annie I would meet her in the lobby for dinner. And, I saw Dale "holding court" with a group of new and more seasoned business owners. They were all standing around him hanging on every word. I was nervous to walk up to the group, but what he said on stage spoke to me and I knew I had to hear more and maybe if I was lucky, I would be able to shake his hand. I remember saying to myself, *"Face everything and rise, Bernadette, face everything and rise."* I walked up to the group and he looked up at me while he was in mid-sentence and our eyes locked.

He finished his sentence and then he said, *"Folks, I'd like you to meet Annie's new rock star Bernadette."* And, he walked over to me and put his arm around me. *"She's going to do great things in this industry."* He had this way of just making people believe they were the most important person in the room. He made sure people knew they were valued and accepted for who they are. I remember nervously smiling at everyone and I looked up at Dale and I asked, *"I know you may think this is a silly question, but what makes people fail in this industry?"*

He laughed his big gregarious laugh and said, *"That's not a silly question, that's a smart question. Look Bernadette, this is the simplest business in the world. People are already hard-wired to share good news with each other; share products they love and products they use. But when they share it's always about the other person. When they get into network marketing, they try to get slick and forceful and they forget it's about how they can help other people reach their goals, goals that either the product can help them with or goals to put an extra $500 or more in the bank every month. They forget it's always about the people when they are building their teams and they make it about their goals instead of the goals of the people they are talking to and the goals of the people on their team. And, they don't believe in themselves. They come to a convention like this, they see "rising stars" and slick presenters and they think they have to be that person or some version of that person to be successful."* There were easily 30 people standing around him, but I felt like he was talking just to me. I'm sure everyone felt the same way because I swear, he made eye contact with all of them before he finished. *"You don't have to be slick to build this business"*, then he looked right in my eyes and said, *"Look, Bernadette, I'm an overweight, redneck from KY with crooked teeth, if I can make millions in this business, you are going to absolutely kill it! You just have to make it about the other person because if you can help enough other people reach their goals, you will reach your goals."*

He then laughed and said, *"You guys want to hear my favorite way to engage people in a conversation about the business?"* We were all entranced and he said, *"It is by asking the question, If I could show you a way to redirect the change you've got floating around on your car floor or the money you spend on that expensive latte every day to create the life of your dreams would it be worth 1/2 hour of your time to learn what I do?"* He was a master at keeping it simple.

Over the years, I had many conversations with Big Dawg. He would call me and just check in on me to see how I was doing and ask what he could do to help me reach my goals. I mean, he had the largest organization in the company and was the top money earner and he still took the time to pick up the phone and call me and always picked up the phone or called me back when I called him. He always made it about the person he was talking to and the person he was working with.

In these conversations, Dale would always say, *"If nothing changes, nothing changes. If you keep doing what you are doing, you will keep getting what you are getting. So, if you love what you are getting, then keep doing what you are doing. But, if you aren't happy with what you are getting, then you have to make changes. You have to change."* Like I said, he was the master of simplicity. And, it doesn't really make a difference what business you are in. If nothing changes…nothing changes. If you keep doing what you are doing, you will keep getting what you get. Keeping things simple, doing the things that bring you joy will always bring you success.

Mindset Break

#1 Stop, stop for a minute when you are thinking of scarcity. Stop working so hard, stop sacrificing, stop telling your story about money, find that place in your heart where love and abundance lives, let that voice remind you of what brings you joy. You will learn to feel abundance before it happens, and you will learn where abundance lives in you.

#2 Listen - take the time to listen to your heart. What is meaningful to you? What life experiences would bring you the most joy? Discover your joy, discover your magical obsession and you will be a step closer to an abundant life.

#3 Act - Everyday do something even if it's small, everyday take an action towards your heart's desire - if you want to help people, help someone in some way, be a listening ear, share what's helped you.

#4 Set small goals for yourself each day. Practice the muscle and as you complete each goal your belief in yourself will grow and strengthen.

#5 Be willing to let go of people who aren't invested in your growth, including your old self. There will always be crabs in the bucket trying to drag you down. They don't want to see you succeed. But they don't pay your bills or create your life. Be willing to let go of those people. You can still love them. You can still care about them, you simply let them go so they stop affecting you, your mindset and your focus. Never let what's happening in the physical affect your mindset.

Obi-wan

I met my mentor Mike for the first time, at the same convention I met Dale. It was a brief encounter. I remember watching him do his part on stage thinking, wow, this guy…this guy just makes so much sense. But I didn't really get to know him until he moved to NH to work out of the corporate office.   And, I really didn't start thinking of him as my mentor until after the next convention. They had asked me to speak at the convention because my team was expanding rapidly. I remember asking if my brother from another mother, Tommy could be on stage with me. I was too nervous to be up there by myself and Tommy was so sure of himself speaking in front of the room. I remember having conversations with him and he'd say, *"I see myself on stage, in front of thousands motivating and inspiring people."* I secretly wanted that too. But, in this case, I wanted my buddy next to me to help me face everything and rise. I had my story to tell and parts of it weren't that pretty.

I remember having my notecard in my hand of everything I wanted to say. I was nervous, joyful and so grateful to be there. I talked about meeting Annie and I talked about what Bill had said to me in that meeting about being a rock star. I talked about the negative things in my past, but I focused on the positivity being in this community had brought in my life. Many people look at network marketing and all they can think and see is they would be trying to push products and services at their friends and family. What they don't get to see is the community of people and how they come together and lift each other up. How they are filled with opportunities for personal development. And, you meet the best people. I met my best friend Candi in this community. I spoke about that community on stage. I spoke about how that community lifted not only me, but my children as well. I remember seeing Mike after I spoke. I was always looking for approval and asked, *"How did I do?"* All he said was, *"Wow!"*

I wasn't sure at the time if that was really good or if he couldn't believe the things I'd been through. But, in his eyes, I saw compassion and caring and someone I could trust. That day, I nicknamed him Yoda. My daughter was very much into Star Wars at the time. We had to go see every new movie and she watched video tapes of the movies all the time. When he found out I had nicknamed him Yoda, he said, *"I appreciate the sentiment, but can you pick someone other than a little green creature with floppy ears?"* Right then and there our relationship as Obi-wan and Padawan was formed. I learned so many things from Obi-wan that I could write an entire book just on the lessons I've learned. I will just share a few in this book.

I spent countless hours in Mike's office. He had a background as a real estate professional, and I was delving into real estate almost as much as I was with network marketing. So, our conversations spanned every area of life. We share a love of music and how it can sum up a person or a situation, how it can move and motivate and inspire. He pushed my buttons and made me angry on numerous occasions, but he made me think more than anyone I had ever met before and in the end, he helped me make sense of our crazy world. He challenged me to dig deeper and not accept things just as they are. He enlightened me, made me laugh and he made me cry. More than once. Because of that, he is my mentor, confidante and best of all my friend. When I was questioning things, he mirrored me and often revealed what no one has ever seen. He always brings me back to me. For that, I will be forever inspired and forever grateful.

The most profound lesson I learned from Obi-wan was to be me. We can't be anyone else.

Don't get me wrong. We can certainly try. But then we aren't authentic. And, it's one of our

jobs to present the most authentic version of ourselves possible. It puts us in alignment with our

goals or better put, it allows us to create goals that are in alignment with who we are

authentically. I believe the greatest gift you can give someone is the knowledge they are not

only accepted but valued for being who they are. When we are our true authentic self, we give

others the permission to do the same.

It's important our goals are in alignment with who we are. That term gets bandied about a lot.

Alignment. It means a position of agreement or alliance, in line with a certain way of thinking.

And, many leaders, regardless of industry want a person to be in alignment with them. The real

key is to not change your alignment to match that of the company or the leader. The key is to

choose the company or leader because they align with who you are authentically.

The other biggest lesson I learned from Mike is about perception. He would say something to

me, and I would spout back, *"That's crazy, that's not what really happened, that's just their

perception!"* To which he would reply, *"Oh Padawan, Padawan, Padawan, perception IS

reality."* This concept took me a bit of time and repeating numerous times to actually 'get it'.

We all have our own perceptions based on a variety of influences. Those perceptions are our

reality. You can take 2 different people in the same situation and their perception, thus their

reality, is going to be completely different. Just because the perception of a situation is different

for you than for someone else, doesn't mean it's any less real for either of you. You know that

old analogy, is the glass half full or is the glass half empty? I can look at the glass and say it's half full. Someone else can look at that glass and say it's half empty. Neither of us are wrong.

Our perception is our reality. There is incredible power in that folks. We have control of our

perceptions based on our view. To change our perception, we simply have to change our vantage

point. That means, to change our reality, we simply have to change how we look at things.

Often times we feel powerless in the situations we find ourselves in. What we need to realize is

that we can take back that power simply by changing our view and our perception. One of my

favorite movies, 'The Dead Poet Society' has a great illustration of this. Robin Williams, who

plays Professor John Keating, jumps up on his desk and he asks the students, *Why do I stand

upon this desk?"* One of them spouts out, *"To feel taller?"* He responds, *"No, but thanks for

playing, I stand upon my desk to remind myself we must constantly look at things in a different

way, you see the world looks very different from up here."* And, then he has each of the students

jump up on the desk encouraging them to view what an author has written from different

perspectives, from their own perspective and to strive to find their own voices. Perception, my

friends, is reality and with changed perception, reality changes. So, before you judge anything or

anyone (including yourself), try to look at things from different viewpoints.

Here is another example that has become near and dear to my heart. Often people look at those

who are homeless, and they pass judgement on them. They must be lazy, they must not want to

work, they are druggies, etc. Because of that perception, they are fearful, don't want to help and

don't want to be around them. I used to say, I don't mind giving a person a hand up, but I don't

want to give them a hand-out. Give a person a fish and they will eat for the night, teach a person

to fish and they will be fed for life. Then, my friend Stacy, who I hadn't seen in a while

approached me about creating boxes of love to help the homeless community. I love my friend and saw a resounding need in our area. At first it was another project and a way to get to a dream I've had. In this recurring dream, I am in a Utopian type of community where everyone is welcome with a huge farm and hundreds of tiny houses, a huge farm-house, spiritual center and more. The dream is clear in my head and I've had it so many times, I know some day it will be a reality. What Stacy wanted to do was different than my dream, but this was a start. I just knew I wanted to give back to the community in some way because I have been so blessed. I had marketing knowledge and knew I could help Stacy with what she was trying to do. And, Oma always said, *"Many hands make light work."* I justified it by telling myself we would 'give the fish' for the night and figure out how we could teach them to fish along the way. And, then… I changed my vantage point. When I decided to meet people where they are, while we were delivering boxes of love, when I heard their stories, I realized that even if I wanted to 'teach them to fish', most of them wouldn't even be able to pick up the rod. And, when I looked in the first person's eyes, they opened my heart and I stopped seeing just a homeless person, I saw someone's Mother, someone's daughter, someone's sister, and I knew in that instant, this would be a mission I would be on for the rest of my life. And, I realized there are different ways to help people 'learn to fish'. When you open your hearts to others, it teaches them how to open their hearts even if it's just a little bit at a time. When you change your vantage point, when you meet people where they are, you change your perception and in doing so, you change your reality.

Obi-wan also pointed out that our perception of what we think someone else's perception of us is, is never the same. So, don't spend time concerning yourself with what you think others think of you. So often in life, we care too much and get too caught up in what other people think about us. And, what do we do? We create stories in our head about them and what they think about us. And, we play and replay scenes in our head to the point that this becomes our reality. It has no basis in actual events that have happened. And, really folks, it's just a huge energy suck to care or spend our time in those ways. Energy is everything. Where you focus is where your energy goes. So, do yourself a favor and get to the point of not caring what other people think about you. What other people think is based on their perception, not yours. And, your perception is your reality. You will always have people in your life who you will care what they think about you, mainly because you have an unconditional love for each other. But, don't give that power out willy-nilly to the majority of people you meet in life. Trust me, it doesn't serve you. It's not in alignment with your goals and it definitely doesn't serve your purpose. I'm always leaning on rock songs and right now I keep hearing Fleetwood Mac in their song 'Oh Well' *"Don't ask me what I think of you, I might not give the answers that you want me to!"*

Obi-wan always talks about the A, B, C's. This is really supposed to be a sales training. But I believe it's a lesson in personal development and something we should ask ourselves often. The A stands for At. In sales, you have to know where a person is at. The B stands for Be. Where does a person want to be? The C stands for Change. What do they need to change to get them from point A to point B? There is a silent D, which stands for Decision. That person has to make a decision to make the change. The silent E, Everything else comes after that.
The key in learning to do this with other people is to first do this with yourself. Ask yourself, where am I At? Where do I want to Be? What Changes do I need to make to get to where I want to be? And, then make a Decision. Once you make that decision, everything else seems to fall into place. When you start asking yourself these questions, you begin to listen to your own voice, and you learn who you are and who you want to be. When you know this, that's where

the fun begins because now it's all about creating the you you've always wanted to be but never realized it.

I've been blessed with many teachers, but I only have one mentor. I do recommend you find a mentor who will help guide you. I have personally been so blessed to have Mike as my mentor, my Obi-wan for almost 15 years. I believe the right mentor will continuously focus you on creating your life and striving towards your goals, they will not have you focus on fixing something about you. They will draw your focus from where you were to where you want to be. They will hold you accountable to your goals and help you learn to become accountable to yourself and not others. They will not point out faults, they will not get angry when you do something different than they suggested, they will not dictate orders you need to follow, they will simply help you focus and ask you questions that will keep you focused on your goals. And, I want to stress, YOUR GOALS, not their goals for you. They may push your buttons and piss you off at times, they may even make you cry. Usually, in my experience that's just them pointing out a different viewpoint which may help you if you stop and try to see things from that vantage. They will help you rearrange so that the decisions you make bring you closer to your vision of yourself and where you want to be. And, if you are lucky, they will become more than a mentor, they will be a lifelong confidante and friend.

Mama and Papa Neale

Do you ever meet people in life, and you have an immediate connection? That's what happened for me with Mama and Papa Neale. I admit I was drawn to Papa Neale first. I think it may be because I lost my father in my early 20's. He is someone I knew immediately I could trust. I mean really trust. Someone I knew would be real with me. He wasn't putting on a show for anyone. He is someone who, even if I messed up, I knew he would not only tell me I screwed up, but he would still love me anyway. I first started calling him Papa Smurf because he used to wear this blue knit hat that made me think of Papa Smurf. After I really got to know him, I realized what a bumbling fool I was to call him that. I changed it to Papa Neale to give him the respect he truly deserves. I met him at a time in my life where I needed to be reminded that all men aren't negative and abusive. We've had so much fun together and Papa is such a joker. I used to sing that song to him, *I knew you were trouble when you walked in!* I watch how he acts with Mama Neale. It's a beautiful love to watch. They joke with each other, banter back and forth and their love shines through. These are salt of the earth people who do the right thing because it's the right thing to do. They stick together through thick and thin. And, they restored my belief and showed me through their interactions that unconditional love is not only possible but something to strive for. I've often thought that's what I want, that kind of love, something that isn't perfect but is perfect for them and is unconditional and joyous.

Over time, I got to know Mama Neale better. She quickly became someone who opened me up to spirituality. She is a Reiki Master and believes in energy work. She taught me how to get in tune with myself and opened me up to a world I didn't really realize existed. We are often so focused on the material world we forget to focus on and take care of our spirituality. When I met

Mama Neale, I was a little lost in that area. I lived in Georgia until I was 8. My mother was

Catholic, my father was Protestant and every church around us was Baptist. My brother Marcus,

my cousin Petra and I were baptized more times than should probably be allowed. Every new

church we went to, we were baptized. When we moved to NH, I went to a Christian Church

(yes, I got baptized again) and as I got older, I started questioning all of it. I had friends who

were Jewish with certain beliefs, some who were Christian with other beliefs. I studied

Buddhism to learn more because I wanted to make my own choices. At some point, I stopped

studying and didn't focus on it at all. Oma tried to get me to focus on it. She would have us go

to Midnight Mass at Christmas time and asked me to go to church with her on occasion. But I

never felt a connection.

Mama Neale shared different experiences she had in her life and opened my mind to the different

possibilities out there. The more I learned the more I not only opened my mind I opened my

heart. She taught me how to sense the energy of a crystal, she taught me all about Reiki and

we've been on quite a journey together. We've taken numerous classes and became certified in

Angelic Reiki. I've learned about the benefits of essential oils and aromatherapy from Mama

Neale. Her best stories are about learning from her Italian Grandmother. She said, *"Whenever I

had a stomachache or an earache, my Nonna would go grab a little blue bottle and she would

put it by the pilot of the stove to warm it up. And, then she would give it to me, and I would feel

better."*

She and Papa helped me so much when Oma passed away. They were the first people I called.

They came right over. My mother's passing hit me like a ton of bricks. Mama would always message me at the right moment. I would be sitting there staring at a black TV screen watching

the scenes of my life with Oma flowing by as I stared at the screen. The phone would ring, or a

message would come across from Mama Neale. She knew I was depressed before I knew I was

depressed. I talked to her more than I think I talked to anyone during that time period. She

helped keep me stable enough to continue working and keep a roof over our heads. She came to

me one day and asked me what she could do to help. I asked her if she would take Oma's dog

Max. He wasn't thriving in my home. I was working from home, taking care of Sebastian and 3

dogs. And, Spirit and Obi weren't very nice to Max. They gave him such a hard time. I'm not

sure what I would have done if Max had crossed the rainbow bridge at that time. She talked to

Papa and they took Max. He became their little buddy. Because of their kindness, Max lived

another 7 years in spoiled bliss.

After Oma passed, I delved more and more into my spirituality. I believe in God and Jesus. I

also believe other religions have different names for the same beings. Some say, it's Source

energy. To me it's all semantics. Pray to who you are going to pray to, just get in touch with the

divine that is within all of us. I've seen so much evidence in my life about God, there can be no

denying, regardless the name you use. When I need something, anything, I pray. I express my

why and my intent and I pray, then I turn my hands facing up and give the how to God. He's

responded every time I do that. He's brought money when I needed money, friendship when I

was praying for community and filled my heart with love and joy so many times. He even

brought me someone to mentor. The funny thing is the same night that I was praying for

someone to help and teach, she was praying for someone to help her who would teach her a different way. I did a Facebook live post the next day and she reached out to me. And, the

journey with her has been so fun.

I'm not sure I would have gotten here if it hadn't been for Mama Neale. She opened my eyes

and it set me on a path that I am forever grateful I'm on. It caused me to ditch the TV. I actually

put a beautiful piece of pottery where the TV used to be. Now, I'm always learning. Some

things resonate. Others do not. But, I'm open to learn new things every day.

So, be open. Be curious. Ask yourself as many questions as you ask others. Know that amazing

things happen when you open your heart. It's how we find what brings us joy.

Marcus

I have 4 brothers. 2 of them are still living. I would like to clarify I've learned things from each of my brothers. They've helped guide me, been my protectors and more than anything else loved me. I love all of them incredibly much. But my brother Marcus I consider to be one of my teachers. We are closest in age and he had such an impact on my life. Part of my light went out when he died. But as I've learned to open up, his presence is felt in my daily life. Let me share.

Marcus knew at a young age to go after what he wanted and to live in joy. He was the most effervescent, happy, joyful person I've ever known. And, he gave of himself, full throttle most of the time. His energy was infectious, and he was a magnet to people. They were drawn to his light. Don't get me wrong. He had his moments of anger and sadness like all of us do. But for the most part, he lived every day in joy, laughter and he was usually dancing.

When I look back on his life, it's amazing he discovered this so young. When we were still living in Georgia, we had a family who lived next to us. And, sometimes their older son would watch us when my parents were working, and my older brothers were doing whatever my older brothers did as teenagers. There were times when Marcus was there by himself. When I was 12, he confided in me that our neighbor's son had sexually abused him on several occasions. Marcus was gay and we were having a conversation about his sexuality. He had been having trouble in school because he was somewhat flamboyant, and he wasn't going to let anyone tell him how he could dress or act. For frame of reference, this was in the late 1970's. There was little tolerance in the school systems and even less tolerance in peer groups for anyone who was different than what was considered the 'norm'. I didn't really understand his choices, I just knew

I loved my brother. He told me what happened with the neighbor's son. I remember asking him if he thought that was why he 'turned' gay. He laughed and said, *"No, Bernadette, no one can 'make' you gay. I knew from the time I was probably 5 that I liked boys in that way and not girls, I just wanted you to know that sometimes I do and say things that you might not 'get'. I get angry sometimes for what seems like no reason and when I think about it, it's really because someone else had control of me, did things to me and made me do things to them I didn't want to do. So, when I feel like someone is trying to control me in any way, that anger comes out."* As I look back, I think it's amazing that he could identify what the problems were at the ripe old age of 16.

The thing is, he never lived in that anger for very long. There would be a burst of anger and then he would be over it. Then he was back to being joyful, laughing, dancing and trying to get others to join in on the fun. As he got older, he did drag. He was so beautiful when he dressed in drag. I had self-confidence problems because I was always heavy and I thought, *"Wow, my brother is a prettier girl than I am."* I remember being a little jealous that he got Oma's small frame and I was left with my Dad's big bones. I think he knew how I felt. So, he made a point of telling me how beautiful he thought I was. I will never forget on my 19th birthday, hanging out with some of our friends in a jacuzzi by the pool of the apartment complex we were in, he sang Joe Cocker to me, *"You are so beautiful to me…you are so beautiful to me…can't you see, you're everything I hoped for, your everything I need, you are so beautiful, to me…"*. I get a little teary eyed as I sit here and write, remembering.

Marcus was a master at redirecting me as we got older. I would call him up, griping about someone. And, he would always stop me and say, *"Now Bernadette, you don't know what they are going through. Try to be kind. I bet there is something going on that you know nothing about."* He was usually right. But it took me until later in life to fully grasp the lesson. Really, he was teaching me to not jump to conclusions and not immediately jump to anger. It was years after he passed away before I understood.

I've always felt like I had a spiritual connection with Marcus after he passed away. Certain songs would come on just when I was thinking about him. I'd have vivid dreams where I talked to him. One time I was doing Reiki on Mama Neale during one of my training sessions and he came to me and told me what to do and where to focus. And, he told me to press down on a part of her leg to relieve pressure. I asked her if I could first, because usually you don't touch people when you are doing Reiki. But she said go ahead and she got almost instant relief.

Funny side story…as I was finishing typing the story of Marcus singing Joe Cocker to me, this song my brother Robert would sing popped into my head. I was ready to take a break and Colby was sitting across from me waiting to jump on his class for school. He's 6 years old and is a joy. He is Kay's son (Zack's fiancé) and I just love him to pieces. Anyhow, I say to Colby, "My brother Robert used to listen to this song, 'I wanna talk about me', do you want to listen to it?" Colby agreed. So, I picked up my phone and started playing this silly song. So, I'm dancing around the kitchen, singing this song that I don't know all the words to… *You talk about this and you talk about that, I like talkin' about you you you usually, but occasionally I want to talk about me.* And, Colby starts singing, *"You are so beautiful to me, you are so beautiful to me…"*. Stopped me dead in my tracks. I almost started crying, but I didn't want to freak Colby out. It was if Marcus was saying, *"Hey, I'm still here, I see you, I know what you are doing."* Kids are so open. We should all be childlike and open our hearts to receiving. When we are, we let the magic in.

As I've opened my heart up more, he's come to me so often. Let me illustrate what I mean. About 6 months ago, I started on a health journey. I was overweight and just not feeling good. I never really had confidence in myself physically. I never thought I was pretty, and I was always overweight. I thought, I can't help the pretty, but I can do something about the weight. So, I started using the weight loss products offered by my company. I had been using some of the other products. Well, crazy thing is, they worked!!! Imagine that, using something and it actually works. I have to laugh at myself because I've been with the company for close to 5 years. They didn't have the weight loss program they have now when I began with the business. And I had been focused on real estate for over 3 of those years. I was referring people to the systems and I was earning residual income with the company, but my main focus was real estate. I didn't even notice when they came out with new products and community platforms and teams to help you reach your weight goals and live a healthy lifestyle. I happened to meet with my mentor Mike and Bill (remember Bill?) walked in. I told them some of my goals and they told me to try the program. I trust them both. So, I did what they told me to do. Well, go figure, I found some quick success.

One day after being on the products for over a month, Marcus started coming to me in my dreams. He was telling me that I needed to do a video and share my story. My whole story. Not just the story about my weight loss. The story of the negative relationship with my son's father.

I remember arguing with him in the dream. *"I don't want to do that, I don't want to go back*

there, I've come so far since then." For over a week every night, he would visit me in my

dreams until I finally gave in. He told me in the dream, *"And, don't just put it on that Facebook*

thing, put it on that Youtube thing, you know girl, I would have rocked that Youtube thing if it

was around when I was alive." I know he would have rocked it. I can picture him singing and

dancing to a camera and a world of people just falling in love with him. So, I followed his

instructions. I didn't really know why he wanted me to do this. But who am I to question?

At the same time and actually for 6 months prior, I had been searching for a friend of ours when

we lived in Texas. His name is Randy. I had been missing him for a long time. We were such

close friends, we kind of grew up together. We were roommates, we chatted about our

boyfriends together, we moved across the country together. We had lost touch back in the day

when you moved from one city to the next, your phone number changed. Cell phones were big

brick things you kept in your car and weren't what they are today. But I couldn't find him.

It's amazing the things that happen when you just stop and listen. In the video I did, I talked

about how my brother had been coming to me in my dreams and how I had fought with him and

finally gave in. I told my story and I posted it on both Facebook and on Youtube. 3 weeks later,

I was checking my voicemail from my real estate website and I heard a voice, *"Hi, I'm trying to*

reach Bernadette, I guess I will try back tomorrow." I heard that voice and knew exactly who it

was. It was 10pm and I was sitting in front of my computer balling my eyes out because Randy

was calling me. I finally understood why Marcus wanted me to post the video. I texted Randy immediately. He responded in the morning and we scheduled to talk that night. When we chatted, Randy said, *"I had to laugh when you said Marcus had been bugging you for over a week. He and Rod* (his life partner, who had died a few years ago*) have been on my shoulder telling me I needed to find you."* I told him I'd been looking for him for so long but couldn't find him on Facebook or any signs of him through Google searches. He laughed, *"I'm not on that Facebook crap, I keep a pretty low profile. But I found your video on Youtube."*

Since then, I've been down to SC to visit Randy. We talked a lot about the things I talked about in the video. I told him that I never felt like the pretty girl and how I always felt like Marcus was a lot prettier than me. Randy said, *"Bernadette, you were always a pretty girl…look at you, we just got up, you wake up pretty, girl."* Makes me wonder if Marcus whispered that in his ear. Still trying to help me and build my confidence in an area he knew I had none. When I was at Randy's house, I found a peace that I hadn't known since I was a little girl. As I was walking around his property and listening to the doves cooing and feeling the sunshine on my face, I made a decision that I will live with that peace and love in my heart in every place I am and in every time.

Marcus tried to teach me at a young age not to focus on the past, to live in the present and try to suck every ounce of joy out of every moment possible. He taught me to be kind, forgiving and to leave judgment to someone else. I miss his physical presence in my life every day. But I know he's been with me for every word in this little book and I know he's just a dream away.

You are not broken you don't need to be fixed

With society's incessant need to fix everyone and the boom of the therapist and the life coach, many people focus on what they feel like or what their life coach or therapist feels like they need to fix in themselves to become successful. That focus actually reinforces a negative belief that there is something wrong.   And, they say things like - If I could just fix this....if I was more capable, if I was more deserving, if I was good enough, if I could make things perfect, they ask themselves, if I could figure out what I need to fix and what's wrong with me....then I will be whole and reach success.

I have a problem with that because that makes the assumption a person is broken in some way. You guys have to understand, between real estate and network marketing, I've met thousands of amazing people, who tell me they feel like they need to fix something in themselves or they're trying to figure out what they have to fix as if they are in some way broken. And all I see are amazing people with beautiful souls who want to help people and want to give their families a better lifestyle. There is nothing broken in any of them. Society has led them to believe that.

One of my favorite and most hated songs is Fix You by Coldplay. I love the melody; I love the feeling behind wanting to help someone take away their pain. But I hate the notion that someone is broken or needs to be fixed or the notion that someone has the power to "fix" someone else.

It's my hope, I help you see the beauty in who you are. My hope is that you see yourself the way that I see you. Because the real beauty and the real truth is that we are all just the sum of decisions we've made, we are not broken, we don't need to be fixed.

Know that you are in control, whether you like it or not! Your thoughts create your feelings, your feelings create the way you think which dictates your decisions and your decisions and acting on those decisions are what ultimately create your life. For example, you can say that you want to build your business or lose weight or reach a goal, you can say affirmations daily, but, until your feelings are elevated and your intent is clear to build that business or reach that perfect weight, it's not going to happen. Don't focus on what you think is broken, learn to rearrange the potential that is already within you.

Much like you can take a piece of wood and with one decision turn it into a bench and then you can take that same bench and rearrange it so it becomes a fence and then with another decision you can take that fence and rearrange it so it becomes a chair, we too have the ability to rearrange our minds to create whatever, whomever we want to be. That's exciting, at least it is for me. There is so much power in that! I can become whomever I want to be just by making the decision to be that person with a clear intent and elevated emotion. Wow! That's the real freedom in life. You are already whole, worthy and good enough. The belief that you have to fix yourself before you are worthy of reaching your goals doesn't serve you. Life is about creation. Ask yourself, who do I want to be? Who do I want to create? And, have some fun with it. Just like an artist can create a masterpiece of artwork, you can create a master YOU!

What people tend to do instead of just GOING FOR what they want is they get stuck in the identity of who they created of "who they are" in their mind. They get stuck in the stories they've been telling themselves or other people have been telling them about who they are. There are a few things they believe that hold them back. They believe they are not good enough, so they don't even really try, they believe they are perfectionists, so before they even try anything, everything has to be made perfect (and nothing is ever perfect), they believe they aren't capable right now so they spend their time collecting things and taking courses that will eventually make them capable (and they never start creating), they believe they aren't deserving, so they pretend to try, but, they don't really even try because they don't believe they deserve it anyways.

What you need to understand is when you spend time believing you aren't good enough, you are not creating, when you are trying to make things perfect, you are not creating, when you collect things and courses trying to become capable, you are not creating, when you spend time pretending and not believing you deserve it, you are not creating.

Today I'm going to ask you to change your structure and your focus, stop trying to fix yourself and start focusing on creating yourself.   Who is it that you want to create? Who do you want to be? Me? I want to speak in front of 10s of thousands of people, I want to be a catalyst of change in people's lives, I want to help people, I want to empower people, I want to inspire people, I want to be financially abundant, evidently I want to be an author too. That's me. Who do YOU want to be? Whomever it is that you want to be, you can rearrange your mindset and make decisions to become whatever that vision of success is for you.

We are all a uniquely beautiful creation of God. He gave us the goods when we arrived here, it's

our job to use those goods to create what we want. I can already hear some of you. But,

Bernadette, this is who I AM as a person, it is my identity. I am going to tell you that you are

going to need to let go of THAT identity to create who you want to be.

But, Bernadette, how do I create who I want to be? Creation is feeding your brain with the

information and materials needed to create your vision. Creation happens with that clear

intention and elevated emotion. When you begin to feel abundant before something has

manifested, you open yourself up to take action daily and go for what you want. Fall in love

with the process of creation, feel abundant during the creation. If the first action is reading a

book on mindset, then read a book on mindset but the real action happens when you apply what

you learned, if the first action is committing to meditate daily, make the commitment, but know

the real action comes when you actually meditate daily, if it's reaching out to someone and

asking them to meet you for coffee, even over a zoom or facetime call, reach out and ask, if it's

painting a picture, don't just get the paint and the canvas, pick up the brush, dip it into the paint

and put it on the canvas.

Bring joy and gratitude in all you do. Be sure to have fun. I mean you are in the middle of

creating your desired life. You are arranging and rearranging and making decisions to get you to

where you want to be. You have to do that with joy, gratitude, enthusiasm and you have to do

that with love in your heart. So have fun with it. Sing if you want to sing, be goofy if you want

to be goofy, and enjoy the process more than the temporary results. Don't take temporary results

personally, they are what they are, you can't account for other people's decisions, and remember you are in the process of creation. This might come easier for people who are artists because they know what they create goes through many different changes before they're happy with the final product. And, though they look at their creation with a critical eye to rearrange things until they are where they want to be, they are not critical of themselves during the process of creating, they are joyful in the process of creating. Fall in love with the process. I like to create things with epoxy. I'm in no way an expert when it comes to that art form, but I find the joy there is in creating. Sometimes the art takes on a life of its own and not what I planned, much like life. I don't fight it, I just follow the flow, continue to create with what I have until I'm where I want to be. What you need to understand is we all have the ability to do this with our lives. Some things take on a life of their own, but if we find the joy in creating, fall in love with the process and follow the flow we can all get where we want to be.

I will ask again, who do you want to be? (This is for you, you are the only person who can answer that question, and there is no one around who can place judgment on your choice.) Who do you want to be? Are you a millionaire? Are you a speaker? Are you a coach? Are you an artist? Are you a writer? Who are you, what are you doing in life? Where are you? Who are you hanging out with? The next question is what does it feel like to be that person? Write down 3 words that will express the feelings you will have when you are where you want to be. Are you joyful, are you abundant, are you in love with your life? What does it feel like? Remember, you are in control, your thoughts create your feelings, your feelings create how you think, how you think creates your decisions and your decisions create your life. Have fun with this, folks, it's really magical when you do!

So, how do you live in joy, lead with love, face everything and rise?

So, what are those practical action steps, anyway?

I've found and hopefully you've seen in most cases, when I've wanted to reach a goal, I never knew the how. At the time, I was just doing what felt right. At times, the path was scary because I had no idea of how to do the things I was doing. I just knew what I wanted to accomplish. And, I chose to face everything and rise.

I'm blessed to have learned that different meaning of the word fear. Amazing things happen in life when that is your choice vs forget everything and run. I believe I was exposed to that thought process by growing up with 4 older brothers. I wanted to be part of what they were doing so much when I was young. I didn't care whether they were playing football or some other game, I wanted in on it.   They would say, if you want to play with us, you have to suck it up Bernadette. And, my brother Steve always told me not to worry if I was afraid, just keep going and know I've got your back. They didn't use those exact words. But that's what they said meant to me. And, I think all 4 of them (Mike, Steve, Robert and Marcus) are happy to see that my path in life has always been to face fear. They all served our country and have said, you really have to embrace the suck, because sometimes, it will suck. So, I'm going to ask you to face everything and rise as we move forward. Instill some carpe diem (seize the day, enjoy the moment) in everything you do. Life is a banquet after all, don't be one of those who starve. As Auntie Mame says, "Live, Live, Live!"

<u>**Step 1 Know Your Why**</u>   I'm sure you've heard that hundreds of times. There's a reason for that. Your why is what is going to get you out of bed when you don't want to. It's going to cause you to pick up that phone even though it might seem like the heaviest object in the room at the time. It's going to cause you to go to that networking meeting and talk to people. It's going to cause you to seek out and learn things you've never learned before. It's going to help you not care what other people say. When they say, *"You're nuts, you're crazy!"* You will laugh and say, *"Yup!"* And, you will keep moving forward because you know why you are doing what you are doing, and nothing is going to stop you.

<u>**Step 2 Clear intention and Elevated Emotion**</u>   When you have a clear intention with an elevated emotion, you can manifest anything you want to manifest in your life. Remember I said I did things because they felt right? I believe that feelings are our internal GPS. And, we have to follow those feelings to know we are on the right path. Think about a GPS in your car. Are you the type of person who listens to the GPS or fights with the GPS? Nowadays, your GPS knows the quickest way to get you from point A to point B. It knows the current traffic levels, if there is an accident that will slow down your progress and when to re-route you. Your internal GPS is the same way. You just have to learn to trust it. You will know you are on the right path when you have feelings of joy along the journey. Be sure to listen to those feelings and follow your instincts, no matter how odd they might sound. Think about it. We wanted to start a polar fleece clothing business. We had no money, no real connections in the industry and my mother was the only one who really knew how to sew. We had no patterns and had no idea how to set this whole thing up. Yet, we followed our feelings and created not only a business where we sold at fairs, we sold wholesale, we had a home party business and we owned a store selling our products.

The first thing you have to do, so your internal GPS will know where you want to be, is to figure out what you want. This may take a little time to figure out. And, it's something that many people struggle with because they have the little 'but' that comes up. Think about this, I've never written a book before. I don't have a clue how I'm going to get it published. That didn't stop me from writing it. All I know is that I have so much in my head that I want to share with people. I set a clear intent and have an elevated emotion. I meditated, yes, I meditated…we will get into that in a few pages. After I meditated, I started to write. The beauty in this is you can use this method for anything you want to accomplish. I follow Joe Dispenza. Be sure to look him up. He says to write it out as illustrated below and then use meditation to tap into the frequency and vibration of what you want, and you will draw what you want to you. Under intention, write a few things about what you want and on the right under elevated emotion, write what it will feel like when it's manifested. choose a letter and put squiggly energy circles around the letter and when you meditate, remember that symbol. So, for me it looked something like this…

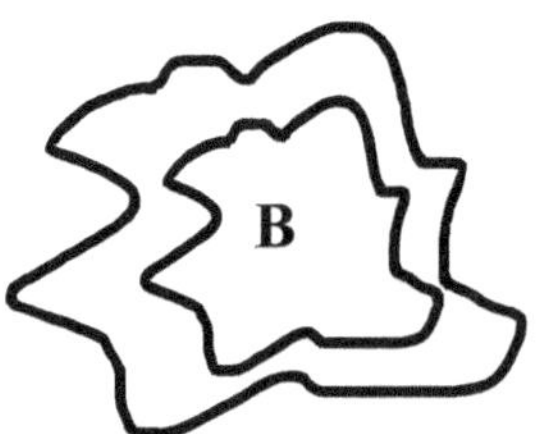

<ins>INTENTION</ins>	<ins>ELEVATED EMOTION</ins>
1. Write a book	1. Joyful
2. Help others find joy, abundance and lead with love	2. Abundant
3. Publish it	3. Excited

Do not focus on how you will achieve your intention. Focus on what it will feel like when you do. My elevated emotion is feeling joyful, abundant and excited. And, I've felt that feeling throughout writing this book. I've told you stories how throughout my life I set clear intentions and my emotions were elevated during the creation before the goal was made manifest. The key is in feeling the abundance, feeling the joy, feeling the excitement. The feelings draw what you want to you, doors open, odd introductions are made, people show up in your life who help you manifest your goals. I have to give credit to Joe Dispenza for helping me to understand how I was able to accomplish certain things in my life. I watched this program he did once where he said, *"People say to me all the time, you're not going to believe this…"* I thought, how cool would it be if I started sharing this with people and I got those kind of phone calls. It's already started happening. Remember that person I prayed for to mentor. I get those phone calls from her. So fun!

<u>Step 3 Believe to achieve and gratitude</u> I know for many people they have to see the results before they can believe. But just because something hasn't been made manifest, just because you can't see the result yet, doesn't mean anything. In the stories I told you, I believed before I achieved anything. I knew, like I knew, like I knew it was going to happen even though I didn't know how it was going to happen. There was never a question in my mind. I think that's why when I started studying this work it made so much sense to me. I could actually go back in my life and see how I made things happen when I did. I never had the formula before. There is so much power for the creation of everything you want in life when you know the formula. One of the fuels to use to help you believe is to be grateful. Live in gratitude. If you struggle with this, write down 10 new things every morning for a week that you have to be grateful for. By the end of the week you will have 70 things to be grateful for on your list. I'm grateful for my kid, I'm grateful for my dog's silly antics that make me smile, I'm grateful to have a roof over our head, I'm grateful for the food we eat, I'm grateful for the heat and the electricity in the house, I'm grateful for my life…I'm grateful…I'm grateful…I'm grateful… Gratitude is fuel for your soul.

<u>Step 4 Meditate</u> I can't stress enough how important it is to meditate. There are many different meditations. There are 1000's of guided meditations on Youtube. Find one that feels good to you. Or set a timer, close your eyes and find your center for at least 15 minutes in the morning and 15 minutes at night. I sometimes have a problem with monkey brain so setting a timer is not always the best option for me. Monkey brain really means you can't get your thoughts to subside. I've found some success without guided meditation when I focus on a black lake with nothing in it, the water isn't moving it's just still. When I focus on the blackness of the water, the rest of my thoughts go away. When I have trouble with that, I do a guided meditation.

Be sure to set a clear intention with elevated emotions and remember your symbol. I personally prefer writing these on paper vs putting them in a Word Doc or on your phone. There is something in the energy coming out of your hand and putting your desires on paper. It seems to work with chalk on a chalk board as well. When my son was young, he had a lot of difficulty with math. All the teachers were using power point as they were going through lessons and he just never understood. We had nightly struggles when it came time for math homework. But when he got to 8th grade, his teacher, Mr. Neeb, I believe is his name, taught by writing and showing how to solve problems on his black board. Suddenly Sebastian started understanding. He would come home, and I prepared myself for the struggle of math homework and he would say, *"No, Mom, I got it, did my math homework during my study, Mr. Neeb actually uses a chalkboard and shows us how to do the problems on the board."* During parent/teacher conferences I asked his teacher if there was magic in his chalk. He just laughed and said it was the only way he knew how to teach. I also personally feel more energy when I write on a piece of paper. I don't know how or why it works. That's ok though, I don't have to know how something works to use it and get the benefits it offers. Same thing with meditation. There have been over 1400 studies on the effectiveness of meditation, in regard to focus, stress, health, etc. Not one of the studies show how it works, they just know it works. If you need a how, I recommend watching Joe Dispenza's 'Rewired'. He shows scientific studies on what happens in the brain when you meditate and how you can rewire your brain. Pretty amazing stuff.

Remember that symbol and when you are in your meditation and elevate your emotion, really get in touch with your heart and focus on the feeling and the symbol that represents your desire. Do that every morning and every night and start to watch the synchronicities that start happening in your life. Sometimes they come the next day, sometimes they come the next week, sometimes they come, and we don't realize it because we don't make the connection until later along the process. Trust the process, fall in love with the process, keep the feelings of joy, abundance, excitement or whatever you will feel with you throughout the day. That will keep your vibrational frequency high and you will draw your future to you. And, let me tell you, being in joy all the time makes life so much better. You will always meet contrasts. Someone will always say or do something. Like my brothers said, embrace the suck. You will find when you do that, you don't care about the junk that's going on around you. You don't even want to listen to it because you know how important it is to protect your energy. You might even do what I did and put a beautiful piece of pottery where that TV used to be.

<u>Step 5 Segment Meditation</u> Some people call this transitional meditation. These will help keep your feelings elevated throughout the day. These are not long meditations. They can be as short as 30 seconds. However, they are incredibly powerful. Each of us have segmented parts of our day and it's important to set intentions for the segment of the day we are in. For example, I get up in the morning, I don't turn any electronics on or check my phone or my email for at least the first 2 hours of the day. I ask myself what I want from this day and set my intention, I meditate, get my body moving and then I write my list of to do items. Then I go make a coffee and get ready for the day ahead. As I move throughout my daily tasks, I stop, meditate and set a positive intention for what I'm about to do. It helps me focus on the task at hand and helps me to accomplish so much more. When I first started doing this, I would slate an hour and a half to complete a task because that's how long it would usually take and after I began segment meditation, I found it would only take me ½ hour to 45 minutes. Think about that for a second. I have been able, in many instances, to cut my work time in half by doing this. Stopping for 1 minute and meditating has allowed me to hone my focus and be more productive in my life. Imagine business owners teaching this to their workers? Imagine how much more productive everyone would be…. It's also made me much more present and kinder to those in my life. Before I pick up the phone to call someone, I set the intention the call will productive, joyful and pleasant. And, because I set the intent, it always is. So, I do it with everything now. If I'm going to get on a call with my team, I set the intention it will be a great learning experience for everyone and those on the call will be inspired and motivated. If I'm going to clean my kitchen,

I set the intention that I will get it done quickly and with ease. If I'm going to cook dinner, I set the intention that it will be nutritious and taste amazing. Imagine a husband or wife driving home from work and they have the stress of their job on their mind, someone cut them off in traffic and they are feeling angry. When they walk in the door at home, they start griping and they bring all of that negative energy home. They don't enjoy their time with their family and their family doesn't enjoy them. Now imagine instead them pulling into the driveway and sitting in the car for a minute, closing their eyes and for a minute, meditating and setting the intention that they will have an amazing night with their family. Work is left at work, the bad car ride on the highway and they enjoy their time with family and their family enjoys them. You decide for yourself what's a better way to live.   I know my household is joyful and full of peace because of this. And, think about it, it doesn't cost you a dime to do this. It's practical and simple to take action.

<u>Step 6 Lead with love</u> This step is really about opening your heart. There is so much beauty and power in this. Some have asked who I am leading when I lead with love. I just smile and say, myself. When I open my heart and go to where love lives before reacting to what is going on around me, it's the most freeing thing in the world. If you are like me, remember I said I'm a Taurus and therefore a bull, this is going to take some practice. Many times, in life, we get caught in the need to be right. We forget to ask ourselves what outcome we are looking to accomplish.   And, many times, a negative reaction makes the situation worst. I don't think anyone wants to make their situation worst. Before you react, you simply ask yourself, what would love do? And, celebrate when you catch yourself. I mean you've been living your life in a reaction mode for a while. So, when you catch yourself before reacting, celebrate that as a win! It's a muscle and must be used to strengthen it. And, once you strengthen it, muscle memory kicks in and you begin living in joy simply because you are leading with love. What would love do?

Here are some examples…

Would love get into a time sucking, negative fight on social media about politics? No.

Would love get upset and let another driver cutting her off ruin her day? No, love would say, *"That's interesting, I wonder why they are in such a hurry?"* and they would keep driving blissfully to their desired destination.

Would love get angry and upset at her son when he didn't do something he was supposed to do? No, love would say, *"What's up buddy, what's going on, how can I help?"*

Would love get angry at a friend who hasn't responded to messages for a week? No, love would say, *"Hey there, I'm not sure what's going on, but I want you to know I love you, I'm here for you and I think you are amazing."*

Imagine the changes that would happen in your life if that were your focus. I was watching a video one day, and the speaker said, *"Happiness is not a destination, it is a state of being. Happiness is the fuel you use to propel you towards your desires."* That resonated with me. When you lead with love you are in a state of happiness all the time. Imagine how your life would be living like that…

Step 7 Protect your Energy If you've made it to this point and begun taking the steps we've discussed, you are ready to create the life of your dreams. As you go forth and create, do what you can to protect your energy. Now, I know I said to embrace the suck because there will be things that happen that are going to suck. It is what it is. As long as you don't let it affect you negatively for more than a few minutes and you embrace it. Usually when that stuff happens it's an unknown. When I say protect your energy, I mean protect your energy from the known things that might take you out of joy, like watching the news or getting on social media or being around people who are always griping or complaining. I bet as you read that some faces popped into your head. Marie Kondo tells people to go through their homes and clean out the clutter. She suggests looking at an item and asking, *"Does this item bring me joy?"* If it doesn't bring you joy, get rid of it. Sell it if you can, give it away or throw it away if it doesn't bring you joy. I know there are some people you can't just get rid of in your life. However, when you learn to protect your energy, you can limit your exposure to them.   You will also learn to protect your energy by setting the intention when you know you have to be around them.

I hope you've enjoyed the stories I've shared. And, it's my hope, those stories will help you to see the power is within all of us to manifest our desires. As you implement the simple practical steps I shared, it's my belief you will learn to face everything and rise, and you will live in joy and lead with love. Feel free to reach out to me on social media or look me up on Google. Just like Randy, you will find me. ☺

Much love and appreciation to all of you!
Bernadette Trafton